MOVING TOWARD MATURITY BOOK 1

Following Jesus

Barry St. Clair

ROLLING HILLS COMMUNITY CHURCH
3550 SW Borland Road
Tualatin, Oregon 97062-9736
(503) 638-5900

VICTOR BOOKS®

A DIVISION OF SCRIPTURE PRESS PUBLICATIONS INC.
USA CANADA ENGLAND

THIS BOOK BELONGS TO

NAME _____

ADDRESS _____

_____

PHONE _____

Produced in
cooperation with
REACH OUT MINISTRIES

All Bible quotations, unless otherwise indicated, are
from the *Holy Bible, New International Version,* ©
1973, 1978, 1984, International Bible Society. Used by
permission of Zondervan Bible Publishers. Other quotations are from the *King James Version (KJV).*

Ninth printing, 1988

"The Guest Who Took Over," page 120, reprinted by
permission of the author, Steve Lawhead.

Library of Congress Catalog Card Number: 82-63167
ISBN: 0-88207-301-X

© 1983, by Barry St. Clair. All rights reserved
Printed in the United States of America

For information, write to: VICTOR BOOKS, P.O. Box 1825,
Wheaton, Illinois 60189.

CONTENTS

SPESIAL THANKS

To Rod Minor for hours spent in writing the original manuscript.

To Debbie Hayes for help in editing this manuscript.

To the Reach Out Ministries office staff for patiently working on this project.

To the youth ministers from across the country who have tested this material and given valuable suggestions.

To my wife Carol and my children Scott, Katie, and Jonathan who have loved me and encouraged me to write this book.

To the Lord Jesus Christ for teaching me the things in this book.

Barry St. Clair

A WORD FROM THE AUTHOR

Jesus Christ has made positive changes in my life. He can change your life too. And He can use you to change others!

Just make yourself AVAILABLE, and Jesus can:

- Help you know Him better.
- Work in your life to make you a more mature Christian.
- Motivate you to share Christ with others.
- Use you to help other Christians grow toward maturity.
- Make you a spiritual leader.

My goal for you is: "Just as you received Christ Jesus as Lord, continue to live in Him, rooted and built up in Him, strengthened in the faith as you were taught, and overflowing with thankfulness" (Colossians 2:6-7).

When that is happening in your life, then just as $2 \times 2 = 4$, and $4 \times 4 = 16$, and on to infinity, so Jesus can use you to multiply His life in others to make an impact on the world. How? One Christian (like you) leads another person to Christ and helps him grow to the point of maturity. Then the new Christian can lead another person to Christ and help him grow to maturity. And so the process continues. God gives you the tremendous privilege of knowing Him and making Him known to others. That is what your life and the Moving Toward Maturity series are all about.

The Moving Toward Maturity series includes five discipleship study books designed to help you grow in Christ and become a significant part of the multiplication process. *Following Jesus* is the first book in the series. The other books are:

Spending Time Alone with God
Making Jesus Lord
Giving Away Your Faith
Growing On

God's desire and my prayer for you is that the things you discover on the following pages will become not just a part of your notes, but a part of your life. May all that's accomplished in your life be to His honor and glory.

PURPOSE

This book will help you grasp the basics of living life with Jesus Christ and will get you started on the path of true discipleship.

Discipleship can be partially defined as:

⇨ Becoming independently dependent on Jesus Christ.
⇨ Teaching people to be taught by God.

Paul summarized the personal discipleship process when he said, "(I am) confident of this, that He who began a good work in you will carry it on to completion until the day of Christ Jesus" (Philippians 1:6).

Before you begin doing the Bible studies in this book, make the commitment to let Jesus Christ bring to completion all He wants to do in your life. Remember: God cares more about what is being developed in your life than about what you write in this book.

USES FOR THIS BOOK

1. **GROUP STUDY** You can use this book as a member of an organized study group (Discipleship Family) led by an adult leader.* Each member of this group signs the commitment sheet, page 11, and agrees to use the book week by week for personal study and growth.

2. **INDIVIDUAL STUDY** You can go through this book on your own, doing one lesson each week for your own personal growth.

3. **BUDDY STUDY** You can ask a friend who also wants to grow to join you in a weekly time of studying, sharing, and growing together.

4. **ONE-ON-ONE DISCIPLESHIP** After you have mastered and applied each Bible study in this book to your own life, you can help another person work through his own copy of the book.

---

*The Leader's Guide for *Following Jesus* can be purchased at your local Christian bookstore or from the publisher.

PRACTICAL HINTS
(HOW TO GET THE MOST OUT OF THIS BOOK)

If you want to grow as a Christian, you must get specific with God and apply the Bible to your life. Sometimes that's hard, but this book can help you if you will:

1. Begin each Bible study with prayer
Ask God to speak to you.

2. Use a study Bible
Try the *New International Version* or the *New American Standard Bible*.

3. Work through the Bible study
- ➪ Look up the Bible verses.
- ➪ Think through the answers.
- ➪ Write the answers.
- ➪ Jot down any questions that come up.
- ➪ Memorize the assigned verse(s). (Use the Bible memory cards in the back of the book. Groups should select a single translation to memorize, in order to recite the verse[s] together.)

4. Apply each Bible study to your life
- ➪ Ask God to show you how to act on what you're learning from His Word.
- ➪ Obey Him in your relationships, attitudes, and actions.
- ➪ Talk over the results with other Christians who can encourage and advise you.

IF YOU'RE IN A DISCIPLESHIP FAMILY

➪ Set aside two separate times each week to work on the assigned Bible study. If possible, complete the whole Bible study during the first time. Then during the second time (the day of or the day before your next group meeting), review what you've studied.

➪ Take your Bible, this book, and a pen or pencil to every group meeting.

PERSONAL COMMITMENT

I, _____ , hereby dedicate
myself to the following commitments:

1. To submit myself daily to God and to all that He
   wants to teach me about growing as a Christian.

2. To attend all weekly group meetings, unless a
   serious illness or circumstance makes it
   impossible. If I miss more than one meeting, I will
   withdraw willingly from the group if it is
   determined necessary after meeting with the
   group leader.

3. To complete the assignments without fail as they
   are due each week.

4. To be involved in my local church.

I understand that these commitments are not only to
the Lord but to the group and to myself as well. I will
do my very best, with God's help, to completely fulfill
each one.

Signed _____

1

ARE YOU SURE?

Finding assurance of salvation

When you walk into class on Monday morning and discover you blew it on Friday's test, what difference does it make if you have a personal relationship with Jesus Christ?

A person without Jesus Christ has no resources outside of himself to deal with the problems that smack him in the face every day. But a Christian can handle any problem or frustration by using the resources available to him through Jesus Christ.

You'll discover what some of those resources are throughout the 10 Bible studies in this book. But to tap them for your own life, you must be able to answer and respond to three basic questions:

⇨ What is a Christian?
⇨ How do you become a Christian?
⇨ How do you know if you're really a Christian?

WHAT IS A CHRISTIAN?

Why do you think God created you?

_____

_____

_____

Read 1 John 1:3 to discover God's perspective on why He created you. Now how would you answer that question?

_____

_____

_____

A Christian is someone who has a personal relationship with Jesus Christ. But that relationship is not something you're born with, or earn, or buy.

Look at Romans 3:23 and 6:23.

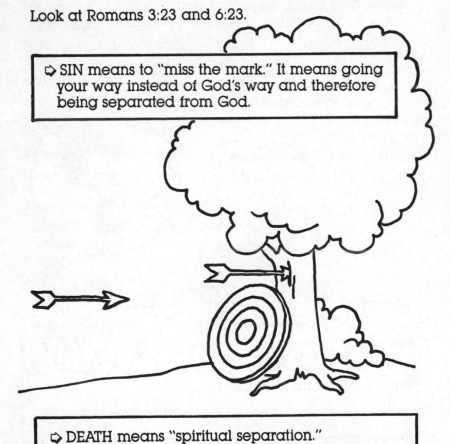

> ➪ SIN means to "miss the mark." It means going your way instead of God's way and therefore being separated from God.

> ➪ DEATH means "spiritual separation."

To solve the problems of sin and death and to bring us into a personal relationship with Himself, God did something special. Read Romans 5:8, 1 Corinthians 15:3-4, 1 Peter 3:18. Write in your own words what God did.

_____

_____

_____

Now check the following verses from the Gospel of John to see why Jesus came:

John 1:4 _____

1:11-13 _____

1:17 _____

2:19-22 _____

3:3 _____

3:16 _____

Read Philippians 2:6-11. Though He didn't have to, Jesus willingly gave up the privileges of existing in like form with God the Father, and came to earth in human form to experience life as you experience it. Think about that for a minute.

So He could identify with you,
and you with Him,
GOD BECAME MAN.

ROLLING HILLS COMMUNITY CHURCH
3550 SW Borland Road
Tualatin, Oregon 97062-9736
(503) 638-5900

Jesus faced the same kinds of things you face:

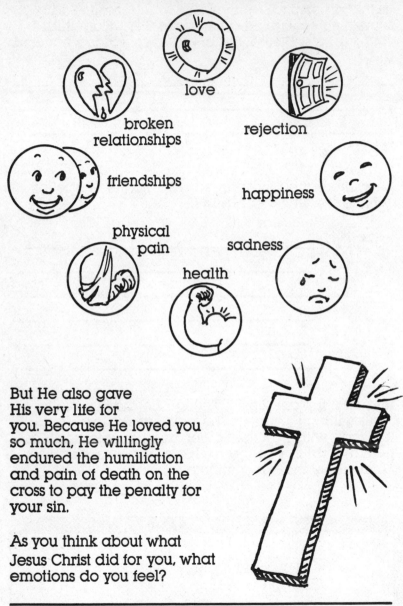

love

broken
relationships

rejection

friendships

happiness

physical
pain

sadness

health

But He also gave
His very life for
you. Because He loved you
so much, He willingly
endured the humiliation
and pain of death on the
cross to pay the penalty for
your sin.

As you think about what
Jesus Christ did for you, what
emotions do you feel?

_____

_____

RECEIVING JESUS CHRIST

How do you think a person becomes a Christian?
Write your opinion below.

_____

_____

_____

_____

_____

_____

_____

Does what you've written agree with God's thoughts?
To make sure, look at the following five steps involved
in the process of becoming a Christian:

FIVE STEPS TO RECEIVE CHRIST

Directions: At each
step, read the Scripture
passages and answer the
question. Then read the ad-
ditional comments and in the
space provided, write how you
have already responded or need
to respond to each step.

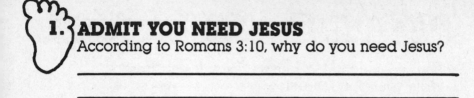

1. ADMIT YOU NEED JESUS

According to Romans 3:10, why do you need Jesus?

_____

_____

_____

➪ Basic human nature is rebellious and opposes God. It can cause you to say, "I don't need God."

➪ But because of God's grace you can say, "I need God." God offers grace to you so you can admit that you need Him.

GRACE is the free gift of God given to help you turn to Him. Grace is God's love and mercy, which you don't deserve. Grace is a dynamic force that supplies you with the desire and power to surrender your life to God.

How does Step 1 relate to you?

2. TURN FROM YOUR SINS

What does Mark 1:15 say to you about turning from your sins?

_____

_____

_____

REPENT means "to turn around"—to be willing to turn away from a self-centered, self-controlled life.

How does Step 2 relate to you?

3. GIVE YOUR LIFE TO CHRIST

From John 1:12 and 2 Corinthians 5:15, what do you need to do to give your life to Christ?

_____

_____

_____

CHRISTIAN means "Christ in one." Christ must live in you. He comes to take control of all of your life.

19

How does Step 3 relate to you?

4. BELIEVE THAT HE CAME IN AND THAT HE HAS SAVED YOU

What does John 3:16-18 say about believing in Christ?

_____

_____

_____

BELIEVE means "total trust"—trusting Jesus with every detail of your life every day.

How does Step 4 relate to you?

5. FOLLOW CHRIST IN OBEDIENCE

From John 8:31 and Romans 10:8-10, what are the first steps of obedience you need to take?

_____

_____

_____

Baptism is an initial way to identify with Christ's death, burial, and resurrection. What are some other ways you can continue to identify with Him? Look up Matthew 28:18-20, Acts 2:41-47, and 8:35-39. Then write your answer.

_____

_____

_____

_____

OBEDIENCE means that when you ask Jesus into your life, you allow Him in as the owner, not just as a guest. (Think of the difference between an owner of a house and a guest in a house.) Jesus must be in control.

How does Step 5 relate to you?

The steps to becoming a Christian also lead you to a personal relationship with Jesus Christ. Go back and evaluate each of those steps to determine where you are in your relationship with Him.

1. _____

_____

2. _____
   _____
3. _____
   _____
4. _____
   _____
5. _____
   _____

KNOWING YOU'RE GOD'S

Open your Bible to one of the most exciting books in the New Testament—1 John. It contains so much about what Christ has done to give you salvation. Check it out.

According to 1 John 5:11-13, what can you know?

_____
_____

How can you know if you're truly a Christian—a child of God? (Read 1 John 2:3—5:1.)

2:3-6 _____
      _____

3:14 _____
     _____

3:24; 4:13 _____
           _____

4:15 _____
     _____

5:1 _____

MAKING IT PERSONAL

If you haven't asked Jesus into your life, you can do so right now. This prayer will guide you:

"Lord Jesus, I admit that I am selfish. I confess my sins, turn from them, and ask You to come into my life. I give my life to You, Jesus. I ask You to take control of every area. More than anything else in the world, I want to follow and obey You. Amen."

If you have already asked Jesus into your life, thank Him for living in you. As you pray, tell Him the reason you know for sure that He lives in you, and that you have salvation.

Memorize 1 John 5:11.

NOTES

2

THE GREAT DISSOVERY

**Discovering God's purpose
for your life**

Finish this sentence:

My purpose in life is to glorify God.

Does the purpose you've written here match God's purpose for your life? Let's check it out.

GOD'S MAIN PURPOSES FOR YOUR LIFE

GOD'S PURPOSE #1

God Wants To Develop a Love Relationship With You

In your own words, what does Matthew 22:36-38 say about your purpose in life?

Love God w/all that I have (quiet time) How do we do this??

Your relationship starts with
new birth as you become
God's child.

Your relationship with God leads to fellowship—a
process of daily living in harmony with God as your
Father. This fellowship can be broken by your
unwillingness to submit to your Father. If you rebel
against God and do what you know is wrong (sin),
your relationship with God is not severed, but your
fellowship with Him is damaged.

How can you restore and maintain your fellowship
with God?

Restore Fellowship

What should you do when some sin in your life has caused your fellowship with God to be broken? To answer that question, read 1 John 1:9, underline it in your Bible, and circle the word "confess."

 CONFESSION RESTORES FELLOWSHIP. But what does confession mean? Take a closer look.

To confess sin means two things:
- ⇨ To agree with God that it is sin and that it is wrong.
- ⇨ To stop doing that which He has convicted you is wrong.

Spend some time alone in prayer right now. Ask God to bring to mind any unconfessed sins in your life. Write them on a separate piece of paper. Then, on the promise of 1 John 1:9, CONFESS those sins by name, and thank God for His forgiveness and cleansing. As a symbol of your belief that God has done as He promised, burn the list.

Maintain Fellowship

Spending time communicating with another person keeps your relationship alive and helps your love for that person grow.

This is clearly evident in a dating relationship or close friendship. It also holds true in your fellowship with Christ. The more time you spend with Him—getting to know Him—the deeper your fellowship grows.

COMMUNICATION MAINTAINS FELLOWSHIP. But how can you communicate with God?

Communicating with God involves two things. Read Hebrews 4:12, 16, and complete the statements.

⇨ Listening to God through ___His Word___

⇨ Talking with God through ___prayer___

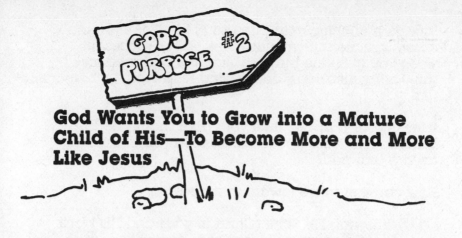

God Wants You to Grow into a Mature Child of His—To Become More and More Like Jesus

In your own words, what does Romans 8:29 say about your purpose in life?

to be like Jesus

Why should you want to grow to become like Jesus?

⇨ So you will please God (Matthew 3:17).

⇨ So you will have a growing sense of fulfillment and joy (John 15:11).

does this love for us change if we fail?

Success is fulfilling your purpose in life. For example, a pen is successful when it writes. You're successful when you fulfill the purpose God has designed for you—being like Jesus and having fellowship with Him.

If that's your purpose, then your goal should be to become like Jesus. You're successful if you are moving toward that goal.

How can you move toward that goal?

⇨ By allowing His Spirit (Christ in you) and His Word to remold your words, thoughts, and actions from the inside out (Galatians 5:19-23; Romans 12:2).

⇨ By letting God use everything that happens to you make you more like Jesus (Romans 8:28-29).

even bad?

God Wants You to Help Others Find This Great New Life That You've Found in Christ

In your own words, what does Mark 1:17 say about your purpose in life?

to share w/others

How can you help others find new life in Christ?

▷ By showing Jesus to others through your changed attitudes and actions (Matthew 5:14-16). Think of some ways He's changing you and write them here:

_____ temper w/ John _____

_____

_____

_____

BEFORE

AFTER

➪ By telling others how Jesus is responsible for your new life and how they can come to know Him too (2 Corinthians 5:16-20).

In referring to the "Law of the Harvest," the Apostle Paul said that a person reaps in proportion to what he sows (2 Corinthians 9:6-11). Faith operates on this same principle. One of the best ways to increase your faith in Jesus Christ is to share Him with others! The more you give Him away, the more your faith will grow!

have you ever told anyone?

MAKING IT PERSONAL

Take 20 minutes to think about all of the insights
you've gained from this Bible study. Then write down
your purpose in life as you now see it.

Memorize Philippians 1:6.

NOTES

3

LOTS OF LOVE

Receiving God's love

Think about love as you've experienced it so far in your life.

In this heart, write words that describe your positive experiences with love.

In this heart, write words that describe your negative experiences with love.

"Love comes from God" (1 John 4:7). It originates with Him. He is the source of love. Yet some people have a hard time accepting God's love. Why? Because their understandings of love are either inadequate or warped by negative experiences with human love. To get an accurate view of true love—God's love—let's see how human love and God's love differ.

HUMAN LOVE VS. GOD'S LOVE

☐ CONDITIONAL VS. UNCONDITIONAL

Man's love is conditional
"If you're a neat guy, I'll love you."
"If you're a cheerleader, I'll love you."
"Because you spend money on me, I'll love you."
"Because you act right, smell right, and look right, I'll love you."

God's love is unconditional
Read Romans 5:8. God's unconditional love means that He loves you no matter what. You don't have to deserve it. God loves you, warts and all.

Unconditional love doesn't have anything to do with how you see yourself, either. Whether you think you're the greatest thing that's happened since peanut butter or a "low-life piece of junk," God loves you.

☐ STINGY VS. SACRIFICIAL

Man's love is stingy

"If nothing else comes up, I may spend some time with you—even buy you a gift (if it doesn't cost too much). But I'm not making any promises." Stingy love holds back. You can't count on it when the going gets tough. It looks good only on the surface.

God's love is sacrificial

Read John 3:16. Look at the Cross. What a picture of sacrifice! God says, "I love you so much that I willingly gave My Son for you." God's Son was His greatest treasure...and He gave Him up for you!

☐ SELFISH VS. SERVING

Man's love is selfish

Selfish love operates on the philosophy, "If you scratch my back, I'll scratch yours." Selfish love has ulterior motives. It says, "I want what I want when I want it." It gives only if something can be gained in return.

God's love is serving

Serving love expects nothing in return, and often expresses itself through the most humbling tasks. Jesus demonstrated such servant love when He washed His disciples' feet (John 13:1-17). That was a humbling act, but He did it to show what serving love is.

God is always there when you need Him. He is always willing to help you. He is never too busy to be interrupted.

☐ GRUDGING VS. FORGIVING

Man's love is grudging
A person who has been betrayed by his best friend or separated from a parent through divorce, can build up a lot of bitterness. If he continues to hold a grudge, he is really saying, "I'll never forgive him/her."

God's love is forgiving
Read Colossians 2:13-14. Some people think that some things they've done are so bad that God would never forgive them. But HE WILL. Remember His promise, "If we confess our sins, He is faithful and just and will forgive us our sins and purify us from all unrighteousness" (1 John 1:9). God's love is so great that He'll forgive us and remove all our guilt.

☐ LIMITED VS. CREATIVE

Man's love is limited

When a young person who can't get along with his parents says, "I'm going to love them if it's the last thing I do," it usually is. Just when he thinks he's got it all under control, he blows up at his mom, then sulks in his room. Trying to love without God's love is impossible.

God's love is creative

When you allow God's love for you to soak in, it will flow through you and out to others. God's love can change your life so much that you'll have the capacity to love anyone (parents, ex-friends, enemies) in any situation—and not just a drop of love here and there, but a flood of it (2 Corinthians 5:16-17).

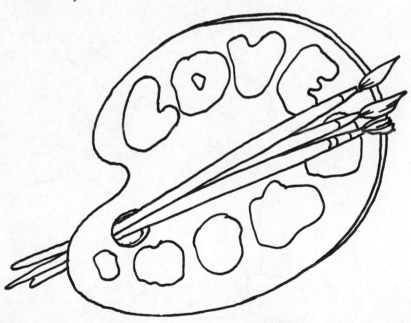

MAKING LOVE TANGIBLE

You can think about love all you want to, but that isn't enough. You've got to make it touchable—tangible.

Jesus gave His followers the two greatest commandments. (Read Mark 12:28-31.)

Now let's examine that first commandment more closely. (We'll check out the second commandment next week.) In your own words, summarize Jesus' first commandment (12:30).

_____

_____

_____

"We love because He first loved us" (1 John 4:19).

God loves you and wants you to love Him in return.

Love should be a two-way street. If a guy dates a girl and finally gets the courage to say, "I love you," and the girl answers, "Buzz off," they don't have much of a relationship. When you fail to express love for God you are, in a sense, telling Him to "buzz off."

Loving God halfheartedly won't do. He wants you to love Him with all of your heart, soul, mind, and strength (Mark 12:30).

MAKING IT PERSONAL

Think about what it means to love God with all your heart, soul, mind, and strength. Remember: God is love. He started this whole love business. And He is the One who gives you the ability to love.

How can you love Him with all your heart (emotions)?

_____

_____

_____

How can you love Him with all your soul (personality, attitudes, habits)?

_____

_____

_____

How can you love Him with all your mind (mental capacities, thoughts)?

_____

_____

_____

How can you love Him with all your strength (physical body)?

_____

_____

_____

How can you show your love for God? Check it out in John 14:21. In your own words, what does it say?

_____

_____

_____

Memorize John 3:16.

NOTES

4

LOVE TO SPARE

Loving yourself and others

Is there someone you're having a hard time loving right now? Put that person's name here:

_____

In Bible study 3 you explored the first great commandment Jesus gave His disciples—to love God with all your heart, soul, mind, and strength (Mark 12:28-30). But Jesus didn't stop there. In your own words, what was Jesus' second command? Read Mark 12:31.

_____

_____

Sometimes a person has a hard time loving others because he has never learned to love and accept himself.

Not loving yourself means that you don't accept God's evaluation that you are a lovable and worthwhile person. If you don't accept yourself, you're likely to look for and reject the imperfections in others that are the very things you don't like about yourself. But remember, God is the source of love; He can give you the ability to love yourself and others too. Let's take a look.

LOVING YOURSELF

Right now, some of you guys are reading this and getting mental pictures of yourselves in front of the bathroom mirror "flexing your pecs." Some of you girls are staring into that same mirror admiring your good looks. And you're asking, "Is that what it means to love myself?"

No! Love appreciates a person for who he or she is, not for what he or she looks like. It means you need to ACCEPT YOURSELF. But most young people don't. Why?

Because of appearance. "I'm too tall, skinny, short, fat, weird looking."

Because of parents. "My parents fight, are divorced, reject me."

Because of a lack of abilities. "I'm dumb. I have no talent. I not only can't play the guitar; I can hardly play the radio."

So what happens? You begin to think . . .

Other people are sharper, smarter, and better than I am, so what they do must be OK. ——And you accept the values and attitudes of the people around you.

I'm miserable because of what my parents did to me, so I'll show them. ——And you begin to rebel against their authority.

God made a mess out of me, so why should I mess with Him? ——And you get mad at God.

Write down some specific things about yourself that you don't accept.

_____

_____

_____

In spite of all these things, you can love yourself!
Here's how:

 1.

AFFIRM YOURSELF
List and thank God for all the things you do like about yourself. Be honest.

_____

_____

_____

_____

2.

AFFIRM THAT JESUS IS IN YOUR LIFE
Realize that as Jesus lives in you, you are not only OK, but everything He needs to change about you, He can and will. Now make a list of those things about yourself God needs to change; then thank God for His ability to change you.

_____

_____

_____

_____

3.

ACT ON WHAT GOD IS DOING IN YOU
Remember, you can "be transformed" (Romans 12:2). Take action to let Jesus change your life.

For example, if you need to lose weight, get on a plan to lose it. Then depend on God to supply the strength and power you need.

4. THANK GOD EVERY DAY FOR THE WAY HE MADE YOU

Someone once said, "God Don't Make No Junk." And it's true! You are of great value in God's eyes! As you become aware of God's love for you, and as you begin to accept yourself on the basis of what Jesus is doing in you, you will become more and more free to love others God's way.

What does God's Word teach about loving others? Read 1 John 4:1-19 and summarize the main truth of that passage.

_____

_____

_____

_____

_____

Because God loves us, we should love one another (1 John 4:11). Go back and think about the person whose name you wrote on page 45. Are you willing to let God help you love that person? If so, take the following necessary steps:

1. ADMIT YOU NEED GOD'S LOVE FOR THAT PERSON, AND ASK GOD FOR IT

Believe it or not, needs and weaknesses are good for you. Why? Because they drive you to God. Just as hunger leads you to food, weaknesses should take you to the only One who can meet them—Jesus Christ. The fact that His "power is made perfect in (your) weakness" (2 Corinthians 12:9) is something you can count on.

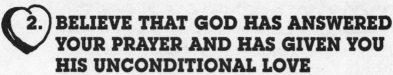

2. BELIEVE THAT GOD HAS ANSWERED YOUR PRAYER AND HAS GIVEN YOU HIS UNCONDITIONAL LOVE

Look at 1 John 5:14-15 and summarize the main truth.

_____

_____

_____

_____

Is it God's will that you love the person you're having trouble loving? Of course it is! God has, in fact, commanded that you do it! So, on the promise of His Word, you can believe that you have received your request.

Now read and summarize Mark 11:24.

_____

_____

_____

_____

Believe it before you see it or feel it. Believe it because God said it.

3. STEP OUT IN FAITH AND DO GOOD TO THE ONE YOU CAN NOW LOVE WITH GOD'S LOVE

One evidence that you're a Christian is that others see you expressing love for your Christian brothers and sisters (John 13:34-35). As you allow God's love to work in and through you, you will begin to love others with His kind of love.

MAKING IT PERSONAL

What are five characteristics of God's kind of love? (If you have trouble remembering, check pages 36-40, Bible study 3.)
God's love is:

1.

2.

3.

4.

5.

Think again about the person whose name you wrote on page 45. What are three specific things you can do this week to show God's love to that person?

➪ _____
_____

➪ _____
_____

➪ _____
_____

Memorize 1 John 3:23.

NOTES

5

ALIVE IN YOU!

Experiencing Christ living in you

GOD

What frustrations do you have
as you face . . .

⇨ your parents? _____

_____

⇨ your friends? _____

_____

⇨ school?_____

_____

⇨ yourself?_____

_____

⇨ your dating life?_____

_____

Now look back over the
things you just listed. Have
any of your frustrations
been caused or made
worse by your own wrong
attitudes or actions?

Since you're human, some of your frustrations are
caused by circumstances beyond your control—the
kinds of circumstances that frustrate everyone. But it's
a pretty safe guess that a few of your frustrations are
the result of your saying or doing what you know is
wrong. Even the Apostle Paul had that problem. He
said, "For what I want to do I do not do, but what I
hate I do" (Romans 7:15).

Paul, who knew the problem so well, also knew the
solution. Look up Colossians 1:27 to find the solution to
the mystery. Write it here.

_____

Now for a closer look . . .

LIVING A CHRISTLIKE LIFE

The secret to living a Christlike life is that Jesus Christ is alive in you.

Always remember that the Christian life is not you doing your best for God. It is being totally available for God to do His work in you!

STOP! Now go to page 120 and read "The Guest Who Took Over." As you read, summarize what each section says to you about Christ living in you. Write your summaries on page 57.

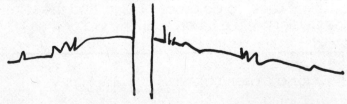

THE GUEST WHO TOOK OVER

The Den

_____

The Dining Room

_____

The Living Room

_____

The Workshop

_____

The Game Room

_____

The Hall Closet

GIVING CHRIST CONTROL

Allowing Christ to live in you daily is possible but not automatic.

Before you invited Christ into your life, He lived outside your life. Your life was controlled by "I" (self) and therefore was out of balance. The result: FRUSTRATION.

Then you asked Jesus to come into your life. "I" (self) stepped down. Christ took control, so your life began to have the balance that Jesus brings. The result: FULFILLMENT.

Then you sinned by taking control of your life again. Though Jesus is still there, He is in a corner, not in control. So your life is out of balance again. The result: FRUSTRATION.

Now you want to let Christ control your life again. Is it possible? Can He be constantly in control? YES!

Whenever you find you're taking control of your life away from Christ, take the following steps.

1. CONFESS YOUR SIN TO GOD
"If we confess our sins, He is faithful and just and will forgive us our sins and purify us from all unrighteousness" (1 John 1:9).

2. CLAIM THAT CHRIST IS IN CONTROL OF YOUR LIFE
"Do not get drunk on wine, which leads to debauchery. Instead be filled with the Spirit" (Ephesians 5:18).

Then day by day you can have the abundant life Christ offers (John 10:10).

Have you taken control of some area of your life? If so, write it here and apply the steps to giving control back to Christ.

_____

How do you think this secret of Christ living in you will affect your life? Be specific.

_____

_____

EXPLORING THE RESULTS

Read John 15:1-11.

What is the key to Christ living in you? (15:4)

_____

_____

_____

What does it mean to "remain in"? (Some versions
read "abide in.") Check a Bible dictionary for a
definition.

_____

_____

_____

What method does God use to develop Christ in your
life? (15:2-3)

_____

_____

_____

What are the results of Christ living in you? (15:5-11)

_____

_____

_____

_____

_____

_____

MAKING IT PERSONAL

Paul named specific characteristics of the flesh or "sinful nature" which God wants to trim out of your life. What are they? (See Galatians 5:19-21.) (Note: Check several Bible versions or a Bible dictionary for clarification of characteristics you don't understand.)

_____   _____

_____   _____

_____   _____

_____   _____

_____   _____

_____   _____

_____   _____

_____   _____

_____   _____

_____   _____

Which of those negative characteristics express themselves in your life? Be honest. Circle all that apply. Then ask God to trim them out of your life.

From Galatians 5:22-24, discover nine positive characteristics (fruit) God wants to produce in your life.

1. _____   6. _____

2. _____   7. _____

3. _____   8. _____

4. _____   9. _____

5. _____

Which of these characteristics need to be developed most in your life? Rank them by renumbering from 1-9 according to your needs. (Let 1 represent your greatest need.)

How would developing these characteristics help you handle the frustrations you face with your parents, school, friends, etc.? Be specific.

_____

_____

_____

_____

Now, based on this Bible study, how can you cooperate with God in developing these characteristics in your life?

_____

_____

_____

_____

_____

_____

Memorize John 15:5.

6

GOD SAYS...

Listening to God's Word

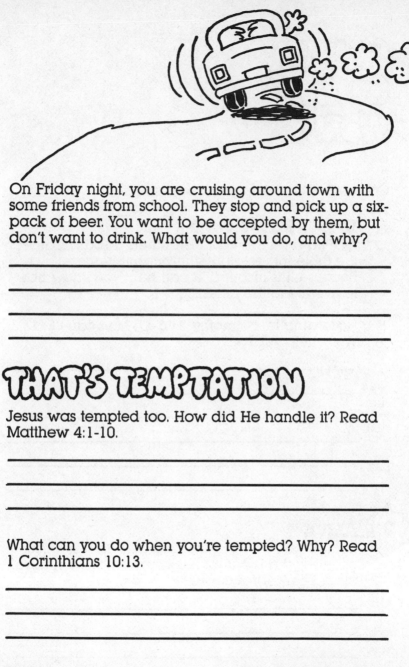

On Friday night, you are cruising around town with some friends from school. They stop and pick up a six-pack of beer. You want to be accepted by them, but don't want to drink. What would you do, and why?

_____

_____

_____

_____

THAT'S TEMPTATION

Jesus was tempted too. How did He handle it? Read Matthew 4:1-10.

_____

_____

_____

What can you do when you're tempted? Why? Read 1 Corinthians 10:13.

_____

_____

_____

Besides teaching you how to handle temptation, the Bible can help you in a lot of other practical ways.

COUNTING ON GOD'S WORD

God's Word can help you because it is . . .

1. INSPIRED BY GOD

INSPIRED means "God-breathed." God breathed the Bible into existence through its writers. Because it is inspired, it can help you know how to live life to the fullest.

According to 2 Timothy 3:16-17, how can God's Word help you?

_____

_____

_____

_____

_____

2. ALIVE

Because God's Word is living and active, it can change your life in at least four areas. What are they? See Hebrews 4:12.

_____

_____

_____

AUTHORITATIVE
The Bible has authority because it comes from
God (John 7:16-17). According to those verses,
how can that help you?

_____

_____

_____

 ### **TRUTH**
God's Word is truth (John 8:31-32). It reveals truth
that you can know in no other way. What does
living by God's Word give you? (8:32)

_____

It's not the dusty Bible on the shelf, but the Word of
God in your heart that will help you know God better
and live according to His perfect plan.

DISCOVERING THE BENEFITS OF GOD'S WORD

Following the example given, look up each Scripture listed on the chart on page 69, and write down the benefits of getting to know God's Word and of applying it to your life.

BENEFITS OF THE WORD

Scripture	Benefits
Joshua 1:8	*I will be spiritually prosperous & successful.*
Psalm 1:1-3	
Psalm 119:1-2	
Psalm 119:63	
Psalm 119:97-105	
John 14:21	
John 15:3	
John 15:14	
Romans 10:17	
1 Peter 2:2	

EXPERIENCING THE BENEFITS OF GOD'S WORD

You can experience the benefits of God's Word by:

➪ Getting to know God's Word
➪ Applying God's Word to your life

1. GET TO KNOW GOD'S WORD

You can do five things to get to know God's Word:

➪ HEAR—Listen carefully to reliable preachers and Bible teachers (Romans 10:17).

➪ READ—Get an overall view of the Bible by reading consistently through its books and underlining key passages (Acts 17:11).

⇨ STUDY—
  Really dig
  into it. Ask
  the following
  questions:

Who?
What?
When?
Where?
Why?
What does it say?
What does it mean?
How does it apply to me?
What am I going to do in response?

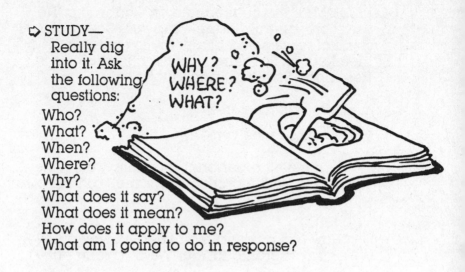

⇨ MEMORIZE - Get started by mastering the verses assigned at the end of each Bible study in this book. Learn them word perfect, and review them every day for two months. For easy reference, cut out the memory cards provided in the back of this book.

⇨ MEDITATE - As you meditate on God's Word, He will show you how it applies to you. God promises spiritual success and prosperity to everyone who meditates on Scripture (Joshua 1:8; Psalm 1:1-3). Here's how Scripture meditation works:

A. Memorize the verse.

B. Personalize the verse.

Exchange the personal pronouns "you," "they," or "we" for the pronouns "I," "me," or your own name. Example:

"How can a young man keep his way pure? By living according to Your Word" (Psalm 119:9).

Now look at Joshua 1.8 and personalize it below.

_____

_____

C. Visualize the verse.

Draw it, or imagine yourself doing what it commands or having what it promises. Picture the situation in your mind.

D. Actualize the verse.

⇨ Ask God to make it real in your life.
⇨ Bring it to mind often. Meditation stems from a word meaning "a cow chewing cud." So dwelling on it and "chewing on it" will make it yours.

2. APPLY GOD'S WORD

Read Luke 6:46-49 and James 1:22-25. Contrast the two kinds of people mentioned:

_____vs._____

Which kind of person would you rather be?

_____

What can you do to become more like that kind of person?

_____

_____

_____

MAKING IT PERSONAL

To get God's Word into your life, begin reading and responding to a little bit of the Bible every day. Here's how to get started:

➭ Set aside just 10 minutes a day for the next 28 days to read and respond to the Book of 1 John. (See page 127 for daily assignments.) Pick a specific time and place, and record them below:

Time _____ Place _____

⇨ Buy an inexpensive notebook filled with lined paper. Each day, summarize your Bible time on one page in your notebook, using the Bible response sheet sample (page 128) as a guide.

⇨ Set a goal of keeping your appointment with God and His Word for at least 10 days without missing.

Memorize Psalm 119:9.

NOTES

7

TALKING WITH GOD

Communicating through prayer

Who's your closest friend?
Write his/her name below.

_____

What helped you develop the close relationship you have?

_____

_____

_____

_____

_____

_____

Developing a close relationship with God involves many of the same things—spending time together sharing:
    experiences,
        thoughts,
            feelings,
                fears,
                    joys.
That's why prayer is so important. It gives you an opportunity to talk with God, to get to know Him better, and to develop the ability to share everything with Him.

Relationships don't develop through silence. To know God, to become His friend (and for Him to become yours) means communicating with each other.

WHAT DO YOU PRAY FOR?

What are some things Jesus said we should pray for? Look at Matthew 6:9-14.

_____

_____

_____

_____

_____

Do you think it is possible for God not to answer your prayers? Why?

_____

_____

Compare your answer with John 15:7 and
1 John 5:14-15.

_____

_____

_____

WHEN DO YOU PRAY?

When do you think God wants to hear from you?

_____

_____

David was a man "after (God's) own heart" (Acts 13:22). Look at the following verses to see when David prayed: Psalms 4:8; 5:3; 61:1-2; 69:13.

Was David always on top of life when he prayed? Look at Psalms 6:2; 8:1; 13:1; 18:3. What kinds of moods do you see?

The bottom line is that God is always ready to hear from you—wherever you are, however you're feeling, whenever you call on Him.

A POWERFUL FRIEND

"Call to Me and I will answer you and tell you great and unsearchable things you do not know" (Jeremiah 33:3).

God is your Friend; He wants to hear from you, and listens to you. Yet He has power, wisdom, and understanding that no earthly friend can ever have (Revelation 5:12-13).

Because He is God, He has made some powerful promises to you. Look up the following verses and paraphrase them so they are personally meaningful to you.

John 14:13

John 15:7

John 16:24

How can you get God's power for your life?

_____

_____

_____

TAPPING HIS POWER

What do you think it means to pray "according to (God's) will"? (1 John 5:14)

_____

_____

_____

Webster says . . .
Accord means in "harmony" or "agreement."
Will means "choice made" or "decision" or "purpose."

So putting it all together, praying "according to God's will" means to pray in harmony or agreement with God's choice or decision or purpose.

How do you know what God's choice or decision or purpose is? One good way is to get to know Him through prayer.

MAKING IT PERSONAL

Do you consider God your "best Friend" or "sort of an acquaintance"? Why?

_____

_____

_____

How does that affect your prayer life?

_____

_____

_____

What is one thing you learned in this Bible study that will help you pray more effectively this week?

_____

_____

_____

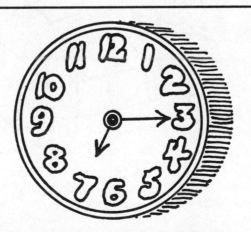

Though you should develop the freedom of spontaneous prayer—anytime, anywhere, under any circumstances—it's also important to set aside a specific time each day to share with God through prayer. To get started, set aside just five minutes each day. Add this five-minute prayertime to the daily Bible reading and response time you started last week.

Memorize John 16:24.

NOTES

8

IN HIS IMAGE

Discovering the meaning of discipleship

What do you think of when you think about a disciple?

- ➪ A big, hairy fisherman?
- ➪ A little wimp with a black suit, black tie, and a sign on his back that says, "Tread on Me"?
- ➪ A person who stops doing 10 things he likes and starts doing 10 things he hates?
- ➪ A person who gives up everything and goes off to be a missionary in Africa?
- ➪ A fanatic who buttonholes all the people at school and asks them if they're saved?

WHAT IS A DISCIPLE?

Deciding to invite Jesus Christ into your life is a very important step. But it's just the introduction. To develop an in-depth relationship with Him, you must learn how to get to know Him better. That's what discipleship is all about.

Look up "disciple" in Webster's dictionary and in a Bible dictionary. Then read Matthew 4:19. From those three resources, define "disciple":

_____

_____

_____

_____

_____

Your definition should include these two ideas:

⇨ *A disciple is a learner and follower.* So a disciple of Jesus spends time learning about Him and from Him and, as a result, willingly follows Him.

⇨ *A disciple teaches others.* He passes on to other people what he learns from and about Jesus so they, in turn, can receive it and pass it on to others.

DISCIPLESHIP IS ONE MATURING BELIEVER HELPING ANOTHER BELIEVER MATURE SO HE, IN TURN, WILL BE ABLE TO HELP OTHERS MATURE.

The Bible gives some definite characteristics of a disciple. Look up each of the following passages, record the characteristic, then write a phrase telling why you want that characteristic in your life.

Bible Passage	Characteristic	Why I want it
John 2:11		
6:65-69		
8:31-32		
13:34-35		
14:15, 21		
15:1-8		
17:20-21		
20:19-22		
21:15-19		

REMEMBER: God is not so concerned about how far down the road you are, but that you're moving forward on the right road. If you are willing to follow Him down the road of discipleship, He will make a disciple of you!

HOW TO BECOME A DISCIPLE

Read Colossians 2:6-10. Note that you are to continue to have the same attitudes as when you accepted Christ (2:6).

What was your attitude when you asked Christ into your life? See Hebrews 11:6.

Your life should continue to demonstrate SIMPLE
FAITH and TOTAL TRUST in Christ.

As a disciple, how do you "continue to live in Him"?
Check Colossians 2:7 for the four elements necessary.
List them.

1. _____

2. _____

3. _____

4. _____

If you focus on these elements in your life, you won't
fall into the trap of "hollow and deceptive philosophy,
which depends on human tradition" (Colossians 2:8).
What are some philosophies, lies, and human
traditions at school and among your friends that
hinder you as a disciple?

_____

_____

_____

_____

What hope do you have of overcoming those
hindrances? Read Colossians 2:9-10.

_____

_____

REMEMBER: Giving Jesus the freedom to express the
fullness of His life in you is what makes you a disciple.

What are some fears you have about becoming a 100-percent-sold-out disciple of Jesus Christ?

_____

_____

_____

In spite of any fears you may have, are you willing to become a 100-percent-sold-out disciple, letting Christ be fully expressed in you? (Check one.)

____YES ____ NO____ NOT SURE

If you couldn't answer YES, talk about your fears of discipleship with a mature Christian you respect. It's important that you work this out before going on with this Bible study.

If you answered YES, continue with the next section of this Bible study.

THE COST OF DISCIPLESHIP

Look at Luke 9:23-26 to see what it costs to be a 100-percent-sold-out disciple. Write what you discover.

_____

_____

_____

_____

Here are some thoughts from Luke 9:23-26 to go with your ideas:

Jesus said that if a person decides to follow Him, it will cost him:

⇨ his selfish pleasures—"deny himself"
⇨ ownership of his life—"take up his cross"
⇨ his goals and plans—"follow Me"
⇨ his reputation and status in life—"whoever loses his life for Me"
⇨ his time, talents, energy, money—all he has— "what does it profit a man to gain the whole world and lose his own soul?"

What do you need to give Him so you can follow Him completely?

THE RESULTS OF DISCIPLESHIP

The cost of discipleship is not negative when you consider that by giving up your life, you actually save it. As you have discovered during the past few weeks, in exchange for your life, Jesus Christ gives you a brand new life full of joys and benefits that you can't find anywhere else. In exchange for your life, you receive the life of Jesus Christ.

Colossians 3:1-17 gives a beautiful picture of what happens to you in the process of becoming a disciple.

1. You become confident that your old life is dead and that your new life is hidden with Christ in God (3:1-3).

REMEMBER: Your life in Jesus Christ is what makes you a disciple.

94

2. You become more and more like Christ as you continue to give everything to follow Him.

Christ is ridding your life of negative characteristics. What are they? (Colossians 3:5-11)

_____

_____

_____

Christ is giving you new qualities as His disciple (3:12-16). List them.

_____

_____

_____

_____

_____

I'M BECOMING KIND, LOVING, WISE, PATIENT, JOYFUL...

What will make these new qualities a reality in your life? (3:17)

_____

_____

_____

REMEMBER: With Christ living in you and transforming your life to be more like His, you will have something valuable to give to others.

MAKING IT PERSONAL

1. Ask God to continue to give you the desire to be His 100-percent-sold-out follower. Pray for more of that desire.

2. Realize that it is the life of Jesus in you that makes you a disciple.

3. Review this Bible study, asking God to show you two qualities He wants to build into your life to make you a better disciple. Write them here.

_____

_____

4. Ask God to show you two ways that He wants to use you as a disciple to share His life with others. Write those ways.

_____

_____

Memorize Matthew 4:19.

NOTES

9

BLUEPRINT FOR A DISCIPLE

Knowing God's will for your life

Describe one tough decision you have had to make.

_____

_____

_____

How did you make it?

_____

_____

_____

_____

What happened as a result?

_____

_____

What, if anything, would you have done differently as you look back on it? Why?

_____

_____

_____

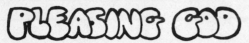

PLEASING GOD

As a committed Christian, you want to do what pleases God. And because He is your Father, He cares about the decisions you make and how you live your life.

God is also your Creator. He knows exactly why you were created. So it only makes sense that you can find real happiness and fulfillment by doing His will.

The following section, based on Romans 12:1-2, outlines how to know if you're in God's will. Read the passage, then work through the section.

YOU'RE IN GOD'S WILL IF . . .

1. YOU ARE SAVED

"God's mercy" (Romans 12:1) is that Jesus died for you.

According to John 6:40, how are you in God's will?

_____

_____

_____

2. YOU ARE SANCTIFIED

God wants you to "Offer yourself . . . holy and pleasing" (Romans 12:1).

Define *sanctified*. Look it up in a Bible dictionary.

_____

_____

_____

According to 1 Thessalonians 4:3-8, what does "holy" mean concerning God's will for your life?

_____

_____

3. YOU ARE SPIRIT-FILLED

You are to be "transformed" (Romans 12:2). That means you are changed on the outside because of what the Holy Spirit is doing on the inside.

Look at Ephesians 5:17-18. What is God's will for you?

_____

_____

4. YOU ARE WILLING TO SUFFER

You are to be a "living sacrifice" (Romans 12:1). This implies suffering—living under pressure.

Look at 1 Peter 2:20-21. What do those verses say about God's will for your life?

_____

5. YOU SUBMIT TO GOD

Through submission you're changed to "His good, pleasing, and perfect will" (Romans 12:2).

Look at Matthew 26:39-42. What quality do you see in Jesus' life that caused Him to do God's will even though it meant death?

_____

Look at James 4:7-8. What do you need to do to submit to God?

_____

_____

Now that you've looked at God's general will for every Christian, how can you know His specific will for you?

MAKING DECISIONS THAT PLEASE GOD

You have to make decisions about the future, marriage, college, work, weekends, dates. Some decisions are big; some are small. But they are all important.

THE CLUES ARE . . .

Clues in Proverbs 3:5-8 reveal how you can know what God wants you to do.

1. TRUST GOD

"Trust in the Lord with all your heart" (Proverbs 3:5a).

Why can you trust God? Check out Psalms 86:15, 145:3, and Jeremiah 32:17.

_____

_____

_____

_____

2. MAKE A LIST OF ALL THE ALTERNATIVES AND GIVE THEM TO THE LORD

"Lean not on your own understanding" (Proverbs 3:5b).

What three steps do you need to take in order not to rely on your own understanding? Read Proverbs 3:7.

_____

_____

_____

3. FORGET THE ISSUE

"In all your ways acknowledge Him" (3:6a).

How can you do this? See Psalm 46:10.

_____

4. IN QUIETNESS, LET THE SOLUTION COME FROM GOD'S WORD

"He will make your paths straight" (3:6b).

What do the following promises from God mean to you?

Promise	Meaning to Me
Psalm 32:8	
Proverbs 5:21	
Isaiah 30:21	
Jeremiah 29:11	

5. EXPERIENCE CONFIDENCE IN THE DECISION THROUGH INNER PEACE

"This will bring health to your body and nourishment to your bones" (Proverbs 3:8).

Look at 1 Corinthians 14:33. What does your decision mean if there is confusion?

_____

Look at Colossians 3:15. What will be the result of a correct decision?

_____

Look at James 1:5-8. When you don't understand results of a decision you based on God's Word, of what can you be confident?

_____

_____

MAKING IT PERSONAL

What is one difficult decision you are making right now? Explain it here:

_____

_____

_____

_____

_____

SOME THINGS TO DO

Using the clues from Proverbs 3:5-8, work through your decision. Be specific.

1. TRUST GOD

How are you going to trust God in this decision?

_____

_____

_____

2. MAKE A LIST OF ALTERNATIVES AND GIVE THEM TO GOD

Write the alternatives below.

_____

_____

_____

3. FORGET THE ISSUE
Turn it over to God. Reread Psalm 46:10 and describe what you intend to do to make this happen.

_____

_____

_____

4. WAIT FOR GOD'S ANSWER
What biblical promise has God given you about this situation?

_____

_____

_____

5. EXPERIENCE CONFIDENCE THROUGH INNER PEACE
Describe the peace you have over this decision.

_____

_____

_____

God may not answer immediately. He may want you to wait for His timing. Use the space below to record His answer as He reveals it.

_____

_____

_____

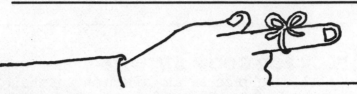

SOME THINGS TO REMEMBER

1. Prayer, the Bible, advice from others, and circumstances will help you make your decisions.

2. God doesn't hide His will from you.

3. You don't have to be afraid of His will, because it brings joy.

4. God's will is not written down on a map that you will suddenly discover one day. It's a step-by-step process.

5. You don't have to throw away your brain to determine God's will, but do let your mind be Spirit-controlled.

6. Just because you are in God's will doesn't mean that all your problems will go away.

7. If none of the options are God's will, don't panic—wait on the Lord.

Allow God to help you grow to maturity at His rate of speed. Don't get discouraged when it seems like you aren't growing.

"It takes six months to grow a squash. It takes a lifetime to grow an oak tree."

Miles Stanford

Memorize Proverbs 3:5-6.

NOTES

10

GOOD, BETTER, BEST

Setting priorities

How do you think most students in your school would define "success"?

_____

_____

_____

_____

Do you agree with that definition?_____ If not, how does your own definition differ? Write your observations below.

_____

_____

_____

_____

_____

How do you know when you have achieved success?

_____

_____

_____

_____

Do you feel that your written definition of success is accurate? Why?

_____

_____

_____

_____

God sees you as very important. He made a great sacrifice on the cross to establish a relationship with you. Because of that sacrifice, His ideas for your success are truly significant.

DEVELOPING YOUR LIFE GOAL

Success means you have a goal to achieve.

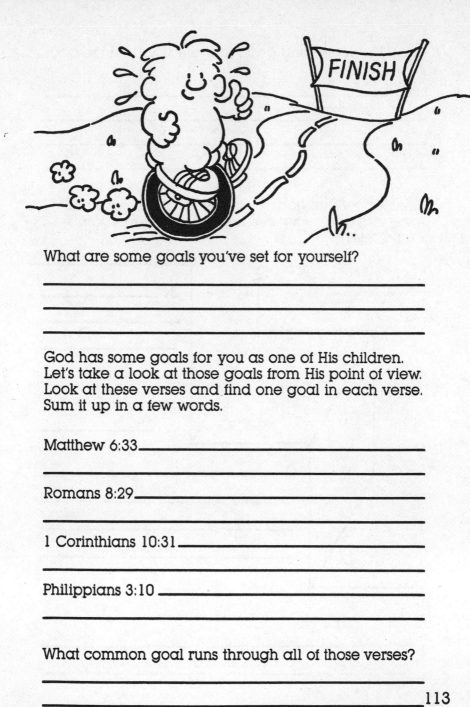

What are some goals you've set for yourself?

_____

_____

_____

God has some goals for you as one of His children.
Let's take a look at those goals from His point of view.
Look at these verses and find one goal in each verse.
Sum it up in a few words.

Matthew 6:33_____

_____

Romans 8:29_____

_____

1 Corinthians 10:31_____

_____

Philippians 3:10 _____

_____

What common goal runs through all of those verses?

_____

_____113

Using the verses and goals just listed, write a life goal for yourself . . .

_____

_____

_____

_____

Think about that goal for a minute. If you set out to meet that goal, what are the first three steps you would take?

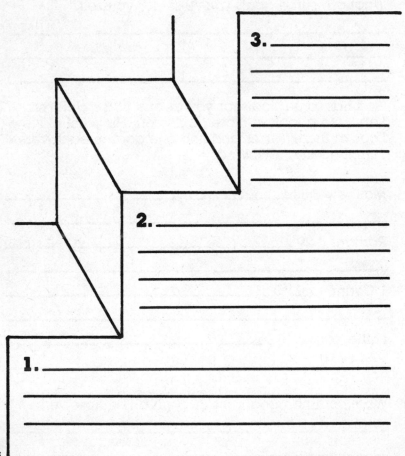

3. _____

_____

_____

_____

_____

_____

2. _____

_____

_____

_____

1. _____

_____

_____

How might your life change if you were to take such steps?

_____

_____

_____

A STRATEGY FOR LIVING

"Jesus grew in wisdom and stature, and in favor with God and man" (Luke 2:52). That means Jesus was growing intellectually, physically, spiritually, and socially. On the following Activities List, write everything that affects you (negatively and positively) in each of those four areas. (For example, under INTELLECTUALLY, you might write: "Make good grades at school; spend 20 hours a week watching TV; read only the comics and sports pages of the newspaper.")

Activities List

Intellectually _____
_____
_____

Physically _____
_____
_____

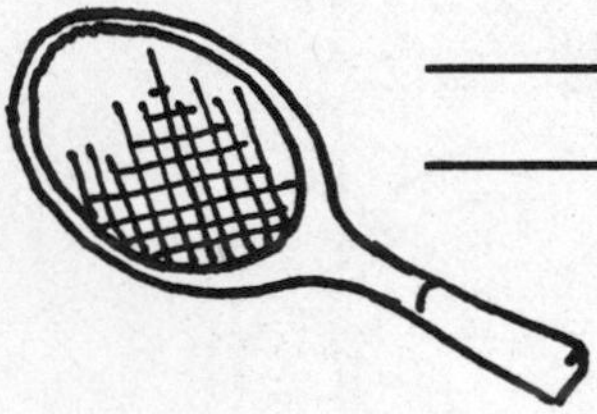

Spiritually _____
_____
_____

Socially _____
_____
_____

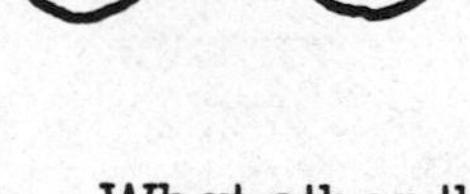

What other things are you doing that don't fall into one of these four categories?

_____
_____
_____

Priorities List

Now go back and look at your Activities List. Rewrite it, listing each activity in order of the importance it now has in your life:

1. _____
2. _____
3. _____
4. _____
5. _____
6. _____
7. _____
8. _____
9. _____
10. _____
11. _____
12. _____

Carefully study your Priorities List as it relates to your life goal (see page 114). Circle any item on your Priorities List that conflicts with that goal.

MAKING IT PERSONAL

Reorder your list of priorities in the way that will make Jesus first in your life and will best help you accomplish your life goal. (NOTE: You may need to add some things you're not doing that you feel you need to be doing. Delete things from your original list that will not be helpful in accomplishing your goal.)

"Christ-first" Priorities List

1. _____
2. _____
3. _____
4. _____
5. _____
6. _____
7. _____
8. _____
9. _____
10. _____
11. _____
12. _____

Now, pray through that list. Consciously give each priority to the Lord. Then give Him the freedom to change your priorities as you grow in Him.

Memorize Matthew 6:33.

If in your goals you write that you want to know God better, one concrete way to do that is to spend time with Him. Make a commitment to continue spending 15 minutes a day with the Lord. If you will do it, write that commitment here:

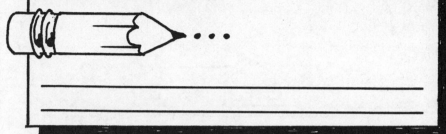

_____

_____

The next book in this series, *Spending Time Alone with God*, will help make the time you spend with God more and more meaningful. Go for it!

NOTES

The Guest Who Took Over

What happened when Jesus came to live with me.
By Steve Lawhead

Saturday, December 6
Today I made up my mind. I'm going to invite Jesus
into my life. Now, I've got a big, rambling ranch-style
life with a lot of rooms. I'm sure I can make Him feel
at home. I've put new curtains in the guest room and
everything's ready. He'll like living with me.

Sunday, December 7
He arrived just like He said He would; He came right
in — added a little class to my life. I'm sure glad I
asked Him. There may be a few little things to
rearrange, but I'm sure we'll get along just fine.

Wednesday, December 10
It has come to my attention that He doesn't want to
stay in His room all the time. I don't know what to do.
I'd never given it much thought, really. I'd assumed
He'd be comfortable there, but He said, "I didn't
come here to be a guest. If I'm going to live here, I'd
120 like to see the rest of the house." I reacted at first but,

after thinking it over, I wouldn't want to stay cooped up in the guest room either.

Thursday, December 11
Last night I took Him to the DEN. It's one of my favorite rooms, so I thought for sure He'd like it. It's a cozy room, not large at all, with deep leather chairs — good for reading and thinking.

He came in with me and started looking around. He went over to the bookshelf and picked up my copy of *Playboy.* That made me a little nervous, to say the least. Then He went over and looked at the pictures on the wall. He cast a doubtful eye at my gun-and-knife collection, and that did it. He didn't say anything, but I felt pressure to please such an important guest. I blurted out, "You know, Jesus, I've been meaning to do a little redecorating in here. Perhaps You would like to have a say in it too?" He replied, "I'd be delighted to help you. But I'm afraid some of these things will have to go."

"Just say the word and they're gone," I told Him. What a relief.

Tuesday, December 16
I'd been planning to have Him down for a banquet in the DINING ROOM as soon as He settled in. Last night was the night. It was fantastic! I had really outdone myself — that's what I figured. The Lord didn't seem to enjoy it as much as I'd hoped He would. Not at first, anyway.

Before dinner, we had some appetizers. Nothing fancy, just some potato chips and onion dip, some cheese crunchies, pretzels, and taco fluffies. We were munching away when He asked me, "What are we having for dinner?"

I told Him, "We're having pizza and french fries, a whole can of pork and beans, and for dessert — chocolate-covered doughnuts with raspberry ice cream and marshmallow sauce. Later on we'll have some popcorn and cotton candy for a snack." I had no sooner read off the menu than I saw Him frowning. "Did I leave anything out, Jesus?" I asked Him.

"No, not a thing," He laughed. "I couldn't help noticing that everything you were planning on serving was insubstantial junk. Garbage, as food. Where's the meat? Vegetables? Bread? That's what you really need."

"B-but," I stuttered, "I like this food. I eat it all the time."

"Look," Jesus said, getting up, "show Me where the kitchen is and I'll fix you something that will put meat on your bones. You've been indulging your shallow appetites and desires too long. I think you'll find the change rewarding."

He went in and made the most delicious meal, using the meat and vegetables of God's will and the bread of the Scripture. I must admit it was satisfying. I plan to be eating better now that He is here.

Wednesday, December 17
Tonight after supper I took the Lord into the LIVING ROOM. He liked it at once — called it the fellowship room. He said, "We'll talk and pray and really get to know each other well."

I thought it was a terrific idea at the time, so I told Him, "That suits me just fine, Lord." And we sat down and had the best talk I can remember having.

Thursday, December 25
Tonight I was heading to the first of two parties. As I came down the hall, I happened to glance through the door of the living room and saw Jesus sitting on

the couch. He wasn't reading or anything, just sitting there waiting. I poked my head in the door. "Waiting for someone?"

"Yes, as a matter of fact, I was waiting for you," He said.

"Me?" I asked. I hadn't the faintest idea what He was talking about. "I'm going out to a party," I told Him. Then it hit me. Since our first time together, I had neglected our fellowship time together. He had waited for me every evening while I went my merry way. My face turned crimson with embarrassment.

"I'm dreadfully sorry," I said. "Please forgive me for keeping You waiting."

"I forgive you," He said. "Now sit with Me, if only a few moments, and we'll pray before you have to leave."

Monday, December 29

Had the day off today, so I thought I'd spend a few hours puttering around the WORKSHOP. Jesus met me at the basement door, just as I was starting down. I figured that, being a carpenter by trade, He'd like to see my tools. Indeed, He was impressed with how well-stocked I was.

"I am very proud of my workshop," I told Him. "I've got the tools and materials you need to do almost anything."

"Wonderful!" Jesus said. He glanced around the basement room and, looking rather disappointed, declared, "I don't see anything you've made."

"Well, I made these." I brought out three balsawood airplanes.

123

"Is that all? I expected a person as well-equipped as you to have done much more than that." He said sadly.

"I like toys, so I make them," I told him frankly. "I don't know how to make anything else. A lot of tools are useless for me, I'm afraid. I've never had the skills to use them."

His face broke into a smile. "You'll learn," He said encouragingly, "because I'll teach you. You just do what I do." I've got to say. He does know His business. I'm often amazed at how well things turn out when He is guiding me through the steps. I'm going to learn a lot, I can tell.

Wednesday, December 31

Big party tonight! We're going to bring the new year in right! All my friends will be there and we'll get it on.

Thursday, January 1

I feel terrible. Last night wasn't a good night and I didn't have any fun. What happened was this:

I was throwing this shindig in my GAME ROOM and most of the guests had arrived. Gossip was making out with Lust on the couch. Arrogance and Envy were playing Ping-Pong and yelling at each other. Drunkenness was standing on top of the TV singing "I Can't Get No Satisfaction" at the top of his lungs. Depravity, with his obscene jokes and weird sense of humor, was on the way.

Things were just getting wound up for the evening

when in walked Christ. I had forgotten all about Him. I guess I knew what kind of party it would be, so I just didn't invite Him. He looked around with an expression on His face like "I've seen it all before." He came over and asked me, "You enjoy this kind of thing?"

"Well, it's okay for laughs," I said. My friends were listening and I didn't want to hurt their feelings. "Nothing serious. It's just for fun."

"Is it?" He asked.

"Is it what?" I didn't know what He was talking about.

"Is it fun?" He looked at me hard and I just couldn't lie to Him.

"Well, not really," I told Him. "I used to think so, but not anymore."

"You want to have fun? I invented fun," He told me. I'll introduce you to some of My friends. We'll show you what fun is meant to be."

I'm ashamed at what I did next. I turned Him off. I just walked away and left Him standing there. I ignored Him and, after a while, He left. I don't know now why I did it. It just seemed as if He were asking too much. To tell the truth, at the time I was having second thoughts about the arrangement.

But my evening was ruined. I didn't enjoy myself at all. I didn't sleep well last night, either. So I got up early and patched things up with Jesus, and while I don't feel much better about it, He assures me He'll help me get over it.

Wednesday, January 6
I was on my way to meet Jesus in the living room this morning when He stopped me in the hall. There was a pained expression on His face and I could see that something was troubling Him.

"What's the matter?"

"There's something dead around here," He said. "I can smell it. A rat or something has crawled in and died in your HALL closet."

Panic set in. I knew what was in my closet and I

didn't want Him to look in there. "Oh, it's probably nothing, Lord," I assured Him. "Let's go into the living room and talk."

"I want to talk about what's in your closet," He said. He was firm.

"Well, it's really nothing, uh — just some antiques."

"Antiques?" He said the word and looked right through me, reading my thoughts.

"Yeah, just a few personal things," I said, trying to keep up the deception. "After all, it's none of Your business." That was the wrong thing to say for sure. I knew that as soon as I had said it.

He disregarded the comment completely. "You don't expect Me to live here with something dead in the closet, do you?" Then He smiled. "I think your 'antiques' are a little moldy and it's time to get rid of them. Let's clean the closet."

"Oh, Lord, I know I should throw them out, but I just can't. I haven't got the strength. Can't you handle it? I'm afraid. I hate to ask, but . . ."

"Say no more. Just give Me the key and I'll do the rest. I don't mind a bit."

He did it all. Cleaned out the hall closet and never once mentioned a word about it. Lately I've been thinking of giving Him the deed to this place — giving it all to Him. I'm sure He could run it better than I do. What do you think He would say if I asked Him?

Adapted from *My Heart—Christ's Home* by Robert Boyd Munger.
© 1954 by Inter-Varsity Christian Fellowship of the U.S.A. and used by permission of InterVarsity Press.

1 JOHN DAILY BIBLE READING ASSIGNMENTS

(FOR USE WITH BIBLE RESPONSE SHEET)

DAY	BIBLE PASSAGE	DAY	BIBLE PASSAGE
1	1:1-4	15	3:15-18
2	1:5-10	16	3:19-24
3	2:1-6	17	4:1-3
4	2:7-11	18	4:4-6
5	2:12-14	19	4:7-12
6	2:15-17	20	4:13-16
7	2:18-20	21	4:17-21
8	2:21-25	22	5:1-3
9	2:26-27	23	5:4-5
10	2:28-29	24	5:6-8
11	3:1-3	25	5:9-12
12	3:4-8	26	5:13-15
13	3:9-10	27	5:16-17
14	3:11-14	28	5:18-21

BIBLE RESPONSE SHEET

Date   Passage

Title

Key Verse

Summary

Personal Application

This sheet may be reproduced for personal use without written permission.

BIBLE MEMORY CARDS

Each memory verse on these cards is printed in the *New International Version* (NIV) and in the *King James Version* (KJV). The verses correspond with the Bible studies in this book. Cut out the cards and packet along the solid black lines. Make the packet, insert the cards, and follow the instructions on the packet. ENJOY THE BENEFITS OF SCRIPTURE MEMORIZATION!

2. GOD'S PURPOSES Philippians 1:6 (NIV)

Being confident of this, that He who began a good work in you will carry it on to completion until the day of Christ Jesus.

---

1. SALVATION   1 John 5:11 (NIV)

And this is the testimony: God has given us eternal life, and this life is in His Son.

---

3. GOD'S LOVE   John 3:16 (NIV)

For God so loved the world that He gave His one and only Son, that whoever believes in Him shall not perish but have eternal life.

4. LOVING OTHERS 1 John 3:23 (NIV)

And this is His command: to believe in the name of His Son, Jesus Christ, and to love one another as He commanded us.

5. CHRIST IN YOU   John 15:5 (NIV)

I am the vine; you are the branches. If a man remains in Me and I in him, he will bear much fruit; apart from Me you can do nothing.

6. GOD'S WORD   Psalm 119:9 (NIV)

How can a young man keep his way pure? By living according to Your Word.

2. GOD'S PURPOSES Philippians 1:6 (KJV)
Being confident of this very thing, that He which hath begun a good work in you will perform it until the day of Jesus Christ.

1. SALVATION   1 John 5:11 (KJV)
And this is the record, that God hath given to us eternal life, and this life is in His Son.

3. GOD'S LOVE   John 3:16 (KJV)
For God so loved the world, that He gave His only begotten Son, that whosoever believeth in Him should not perish, but have everlasting life.

4. LOVING OTHERS 1 John 3:23 (KJV)
And this is His commandment, that we should believe on the name of His Son Jesus Christ, and love one another, as He gave us commandment.

5. CHRIST IN YOU   John 15:5 (KJV)
I am the vine, ye are the branches. He that abideth in Me, and I in him, the same bringeth forth much fruit: for without Me ye can do nothing.

6. GOD'S WORD   Psalm 119:9 (KJV)
Wherewithal shall a young man cleanse his way? By taking heed thereto according to Thy Word.

7. PRAYER   *John 16:24 (KJV)*

Hitherto have ye asked nothing in My name. Ask, and ye shall receive, that your joy may be full.

8. DISCIPLESHIP *Matthew 4:19 (KJV)*

And He saith unto them, "Follow Me, and I will make you fishers of men."

9. GOD'S WILL *Proverbs 3:5-6 (KJV)*

Trust in the Lord with all thine heart; and lean not unto thine own understanding. In all thy ways acknowledge Him, and He shall direct thy paths.

10. PRIORITIES *Matthew 6:33 (KJV)*

But seek ye first the kingdom of God, and His righteousness; and all these things shall be added unto you.

PACKET FOR CARDS

▷ Cut out.
▷ Fold *in* on dotted lines.
▷ Tape short flap to back on outside edges.

INSTRUCTIONS:

✧ Always carry this packet with you.
✧ Memorize a verse a week.
✧ Daily review each verse you've learned.
✧ Have someone check your progress each week.
✧ Apply each verse to your daily life.

7. PRAYER John 16:24 (NIV)
Until now you have not asked for anything in My name. Ask and you will receive, and your joy will be complete.

8. DISCIPLESHIP Matthew 4:19 (NIV)
"Come, follow Me," Jesus said, "and I will make you fishers of men."

9. GOD'S WILL Proverbs 3:5-6 (NIV)
Trust in the Lord with all your heart and lean not on your own understanding; in all your ways acknowledge Him, and He will make your paths straight.

10. PRIORITIES Matthew 6:33 (NIV)
But seek first His kingdom and His righteousness, and all these things will be given to you as well.